St. Mark's Basilica

by Maria Da Villa Urbani

© Copyright Kina Italia S.p.A., Milan
Text: Maria Da Villa Urbani
Photographs: Kina Italia Archives, Pianeta Immagine, St. Mark's Procuratorate
Photographs on pp. 44, 45, 64, 65, 66, 67, 78, 79, 80 and 81 by Mario Carrieri
Page lay-out: Renzo Matino
Printers: Kina Italia S.p.A., Milan
All rights to photographs and text reserved.

ST. MARK'S BASILICA

History

St. Mark's Basilica, *a place of worship and historical association for Venetians, is without a doubt the leading symbol of the city of Venice, attracting visitors from far and wide because of its special charm and wealth of Oriental features.*

St. Mark's Church was the Dukes' Chapel until the end of the 18th century, and is therefore imbued with centuries of the civil and religious history of the Venetian Republic. Since 1807, when it became the city's cathedral instead of S. Pietro di Castello, it has welcomed worshippers from Venice and all over the world. Its bishop holds the ancient title of Patriarch.

The first St. Mark's church, designed as the saint's martyrium (sepulchre) by Doge Giustiniano Particiaco, was built in the north-western corner of the ancient Ducal Palace after 828, when St. Mark's body, having been rescued from profanation, was shipped by the Venetians from Alexandria to Venice.

There are a number of widely differing hypotheses about the shape of the original Church, based on the few archeological finds, the walls, and comparison with contemporary church design. The only point the experts agree on is that it was smaller than the present building. The first St. Mark's may have had a Roman basilica or a Greek cross plan, or it may have been a centrally-planned building whose structure was modified to become the present crypt.

In 976 it was largely destroyed by a fire which spread from the Ducal Palace to the Church during an uprising against Doge Candiano IV, who tyrannised the city. It was immediately restored by Doge St. Pietro Orseolo I. But it was not until 1063, under Doge Domenico Contarini, that an unknown architect, probably Greek, started work on a much bigger church than the previous one, modelled on the Twelve apostles' Basilica in Constantinople.

The new structure, which incorporated the ancient foundations and walls, had a Greek cross plan, although the size of the transept was limited by the existing buildings (the ancient castle to the south and St. Theodore's Church to the north). Five large cupolas were built on the arms of the cross and at their point of intersection.

On 8th October 1094, when Vitale Falier was Doge, St. Mark's body was given its final burial in a marble arch in the centre of the crypt under the high altar in the presbytery, and the Church was consecrated.

The extensive mosaic decoration, imitating a Byzantine model, which covers the upper part of the structure, was perhaps started as early as 1071 during the Dogeship of Domenico Selvo, as recounted by the chroniclers of the day, but it was not until the 12th century that the basic core of the iconographic plan of the interior was constructed. Mosaics were laid in the atrium in the 13th century and in the Baptistry and St. Isidore's Chapel in the 14th century. Later additions were the mosaics in the Mascoli Chapel (15th century) and the Sacristy (16th century). Work continued on the mosaics in later

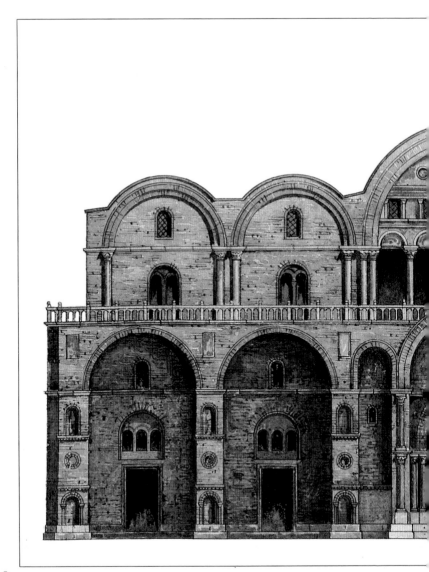

centuries, and parts which had deteriorated or fallen were frequently replaced.

The Basilica was a "living body" throughout its centuries of history. Modified, enlarged, marble-clad and decorated with columns and statues, it features styles of both Oriental and Western origin which make it a very unusual blend of artistic elements. At the turn of the century English writer John Ruskin called it "a precious reliquary, an illuminated gold and alabaster prayer book".

Hypothetical reconstruction of the Basilica façade called the Contarini façade, early 13th century (Aquarel by A. Pellanda 19th century)

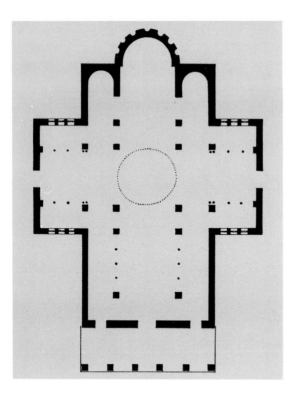

The great civil ceremonies of Venice were celebrated in St. Mark's Church. Here the Doge was presented to the city after his election in the Ducal Palace, here Popes, sovereigns and foreign ambassadors were received, and here "sea captains" came to ask protection before setting off on their expeditions. The floor of the atrium in front of the central portal portrays the meeting of reconciliation held in 1177 between Frederick Barbarossa and Pope Alexander III under the auspices of Doge Sebastiano Ziani.

St. Mark's was also a meeting place and place of worship for Venetians in times of crisis, such as in 1576 when a vow was made to erect a temple to Christ the Redeemer, in 1630 when a vow was made to the Virgin Mary to obtain release from two terrible plagues, and lastly in 1797, when Venice's independence came to an end.

The exterior

Seen from the outside, the most outstanding feature of the upper part of St. Mark's Basilica is the profile of the raised **cupolas**, lead-covered wooden constructions which were overlaid on the brick cupolas of the Contarini church in the 13th century. Small cupolas crowned by cosmic crosses with gilded spheres are built on them.

The lower part of the building, in which the brickwork was originally designed to remain exposed, was subsequently marble-clad along the sides where the three façades open up in a very unitary design. The idea of covering the three façades with marble occurred to the Venetians after the

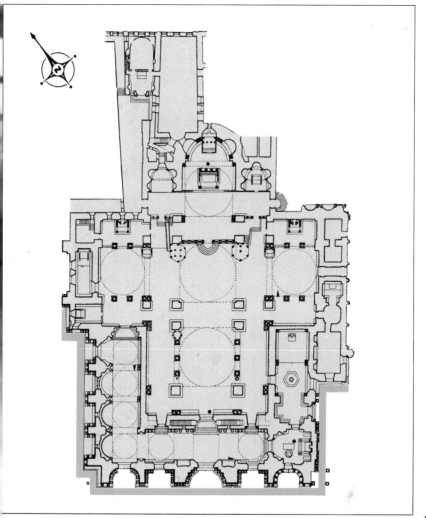

conquest of Constantinople in 1204, when a large amount of precious oriental marble, columns and capitals belonging to sacred and profane buildings in the capital of the Roman Empire of the East became available.

The main **west façade** is divided into two orders by the terrace, on which stand four horses with triumphal significance, also brought from Constantinople (these horses are copies, the originals being housed in St. Mark's Museum). In each of the two orders there are five large arches, corresponding

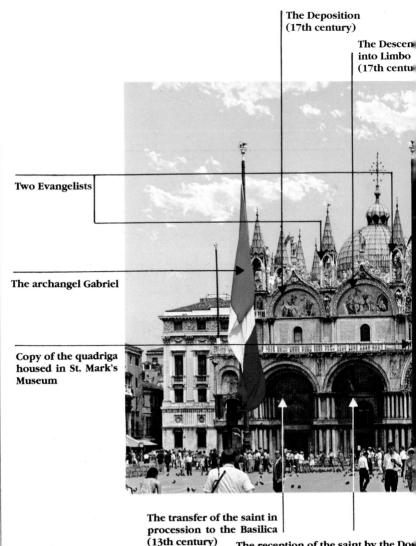

The Deposition (17th century)

The Descen into Limbo (17th centu

Two Evangelists

The archangel Gabriel

Copy of the quadriga housed in St. Mark's Museum

The transfer of the saint in procession to the Basilica (13th century)

The reception of the saint by the Dog and nobility (18th century)

in the lower order to the four entrances to the atrium and the window of the Zen Chapel (last arch on the right). The most noteworthy of the **bronze portals** are the principal one, a 13th century adaptation of two very ancient Byzantine doors (5th or 6th century) decorated with arches, and the second from the left, a portal of Venetian manufacture which repeats the arch pattern and is engraved with the date (1300) and the signature of the goldsmith Bertuccio, who probably also made the other portals.

The 13th-century marble cladding is inset with

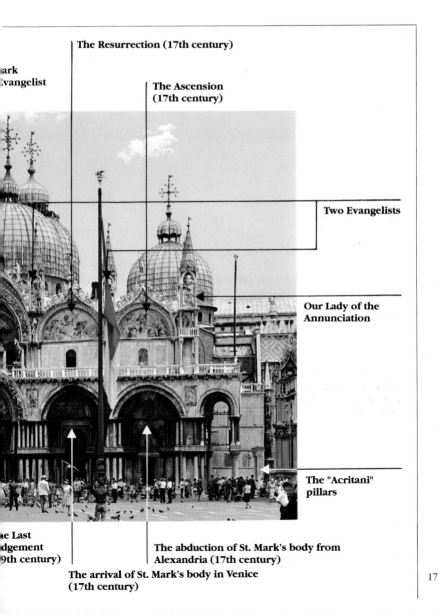

The Resurrection (17th century)

ark
vangelist

The Ascension
(17th century)

Two Evangelists

Our Lady of the
Annunciation

The "Acritani"
pillars

e Last
dgement
9th century)

The abduction of St. Mark's body from
Alexandria (17th century)

The arrival of St. Mark's body in Venice
(17th century)

2) Bowl vault above St. Alipio's portal: *The transfer of St. Mark in procession to the Basilica.* (The only ancient mosaic on the main façade, 13th century).

Byzantine relief carvings, designed to be viewed in pairs on either side of the main portal. The reliefs on either side of the portal depict two holy warriors, *St. George and St. Demetrius*, whose function of defence against evil is evident. The next panel on the right shows the *archangel Gabriel*, while its counterpart on the left portrays the *Virgin Mary*; together they illustrate the *Annunciation*. This Christian feast has always been celebrated with particular solemnity in Venice, because the ancient chronicles record that the city was founded on 25th March (the Feast of the Annunciation) in the year 421.

Finally, the two panels depicting the *labours of Hercules* at either end of the façade are a good

2

example of how pagan subjects were transformed into Christian themes in the Middle Ages; the mythological story of Hercules conquering the strength of animals became an allegory for Christian salvation.

The sculptures on the undersides of the three arches surrounding the **central portal,** masterpieces by 13th-century Venetian artists trained in the Byzantine school, who gradually absorbed Western influences from France and the Po Valley, should be considered as a separate nucleus. Sacred and profane themes, including some specifically Venetian subjects, intersect on the soffits and faces. The second soffit, showing the months and signs of the zodiac, and the

3) Upper order of the main façade: *The Horses of St. Mark*. The original gilded bronze quadriga shown here is now housed in St. Mark's Museum, and has been replaced with copies.

third soffit, showing various trades, with fishermen and "squeraroli" (boat-builders) portrayed alongside activities common to other towns, are exceptionally beautiful.

All that remains of the ancient mosaics executed during the 13th century is the first on the left above St. Alipio's portal. All the others were restored in the 17th and 18th centuries, but still follow the original iconographic plan. In order to understand their message, they should be viewed starting with the soffit and lunette above the first portal on the right portraying the *abduction of St. Mark's body from Alexandria*. Moving towards the left, the *arrival of St. Mark's body in Venice, its reception by the Doge and*

nobility, and *the translation of the saint in procession to the Basilica* can be seen above the other portals.

The lower register of mosaics celebrates the presence of the remains of St. Mark in Venice and in the Basilica.

The scheme is completed by the 4 lunettes in the upper register depicting the final mysteries in the life of Jesus: beginning from the left, these are *the deposition from the cross, the descent to hell, the Resurrection* and *the Ascension.* In the centre, above the main portal, is the eschatological vision of *the last coming of Christ the judge,* portrayed in a mosaic restored in the 1830s. Taken together, the mosaics express the message of salvation brought by Jesus

4) St. Mark's basilica: view of the south façade, toward the Piazzetta, and the old *porta da mar.*

and preached among the lagoons by Mark the evangelist, anticipating the themes later elaborated on by the mosaics in the interior.

In the 14th and 15th centuries Nicolò and Pietro Lamberti and other Tuscan artists added the Gothic "crowning", with "inhabited" niches, statues and floral decorations.

The scene of the *Annunciation* is repeated in the end niches, with the archangel Gabriel on the left and the Virgin Mary on the right, both kneeling. The inner niches portray the four evangelists with their symbols the angel, the lion, the eagle and the bull. Below each one a waterspout in the shape of a man collects and pours out rainwater. The symbolic allusion of the

4

water cascading below the evangelists to Baptismal water is clear.

Four warrior saints are depicted above the "floral" arches, in their role of protectors against the enemy. Surmounting the largest arch, dominating the square and the city, is St. Mark in the act of giving his blessing, with incense-bearing angels rising towards him. In the centre of the star-spangled mosaic below is the lion with open book and the words *Pax tibi Marce, evangelista meus (Peace be unto you Mark, my evangelist).*

The two corner elements mark the passage to the north and south side façades.

The **south façade** is the most interesting one. It once

5) Porphyry sculpture originating from Constantinople: *The Tetrarchs or Moors* (4th century Egyptian art).

5

6) North façade towards Piazzetta "dei Leoncini": the "Porta dei Fiori" (late 13th century). A relief Nativity Scene is enclosed in the lower arch.

contained the "sea gate", the great portal which led through a corridor into the western atrium directly from the quay. After the 16th century this opening was closed by a marble transenna for the construction of the **Zen Chapel** in the interior (see p. 96).

The terrace, with two orders of arches, continues on this side. There are few mosaic inserts, consisting of single figures of saints and a praying Madonna. Marble cladding and columns with numerous fragments of decoration, again dating from the 13th century, also envelop the massive architecture of the **Treasury**, situated between the Basilica and the Ducal palace. On the corner is the porphyry sculpture of the *Tetrarchs, or Moors* (4th century). The Gothic "crowning" is also in evidence, with figures of saints in niches and figures of virtues above the arches.

In front of the Baptistry door are two richly decorated **pillars**, called "acritani" because they were believed to originate from St. John of Acri in Syria, although they were actually part of the booty taken from Constantinople.

The **north façade** overlooks Piazzetta S. Basso or "dei Leoncini". It has the same design as the other two, and although it appears less rich in decorative elements it retains some very attractive 13th century sculpted panels (*Christ and the four evangelists*) near the **Porta dei Fiori**. This door is surmounted by an elegant sculpture with a *nativity scene* bordered by two soffits carved with angels and prophets (late 13th century).

The Gothic "crowning" continues on top, with floral decorations and figures of virtues and fathers of the Church.

St. Mark the Evangelist

The few historical facts about St. Mark the evangelist are traditionally supplemented by quotes from the Epistles of Peter and Paul and the Acts of the apostles. Mark, a Judeo-Christian from Jerusalem, was one of the leading apostles immediately after the death of Jesus. Together with Barnabas he followed Paul in his itinerant preaching for a while, then settled at Alexandria in Egypt, becoming the first bishop of the Christian community there. He later returned to Rome to join Peter, who in a letter called him "son". Mark's Gospel, considered the oldest of the four, is believed to have been written in Rome shortly after 50 A.D., at the request of Peter or the Christian community, who wished to retain a record of Peter's preachings. Mark later returned to Alexandria, where he was martyred on 25th April in 68 A.D..

It was only in the 8th and 9th centuries that the legend of St. Mark's preaching in the Venice lagoon area was fully formulated, especially in the Roman town of Aquileia, which gloried in founding its Christian faith on conversion by St. Mark. The first bishop of Aquileia is believed to have been his disciple Ermagora, taken by Mark to Rome to be consecrated by Peter.

The legend, which originated in Aquileia, acquired more details following the claims advanced by Grado, and in the centuries around the year 1000 it became Venetian.

In fact, the body of St. Mark had been shipped in 828 from Alexandria to Venice, which was then developing in financial and political terms in competition with Aquileia.

Two Venetian merchants, Buono da Malamocco and Rustico da Torcello, had travelled to Alexandria on business, and went to venerate the saint's relics in the Church dedicated to him. There they were told by the monk Staurazio and the priest Teodoro, custodians of the temple, that the church had been profaned by the Muslims, who were plundering Christian churches to build mosques. The two merchants removed the remains of St. Mark and concealed them in baskets of vegetables and pork, at the sight of which the Arabs fled crying "kanzir, kanzir!" (pork, pork!). After a voyage full of dangers which were miraculously overcome, the body of the saint was received by Doge Giustiniano Particiaco, who immediately ordered the construction of a church as St. Mark's martyrium (all these episodes are portrayed in the mosaics on the vaults at the sides of the presbytery, the soffits in the façade and the small enamels in the "Pala d'oro").

Venetian legend also narrates the "dream" of St. Mark. During the voyage among the lagoons, he is said to have seen in his sleep an angel who announced "Peace be unto you, Mark, for here your body will find rest after death" (mosaics in the Zen Chapel).

The "Inventio" or rediscovery of St. Mark's body is the last episode in the Venetian legend. During the construction of the third basilica, the saint's remains had been so well hidden that some years later, on the death of the Doge and the primicerius, no-one knew where to find them. It was not until 1094, after days of intensive prayer by Doge Vitale Falier, the patriarch, and the entire population, that the relics miraculously reappeared inside a pillar (mosaic in south transept).

Religious and civil values were blended and enhanced in the cult of St. Mark in Venice. The city was identified throughout its centuries of history with the symbol of the winged lion, which Christian tradition associates with the image of St. Mark the evangelist. Its banners, churches, palaces, ships and the lands it conquered were all marked with the lion symbol.

The atrium

Access is gained from the Square to the Church
through the atrium. Especially in the afternoon, when
the sunlight penetrates through the large barrel vault
in the façade, the atrium is illuminated by the gleam
of gold from the mosaics, giving the unhurried visitor
a foretaste of the holiness of the interior.
The atrium, built a century after the rest of the
church, was decorated during the 13th century with
mosaics covering the small cupolas, vaults and
lunettes. These mosaics were the exquisite product of
a workshop consisting entirely of Venetian mosaic
makers.
A detailed Old Testament story, chosen from the book

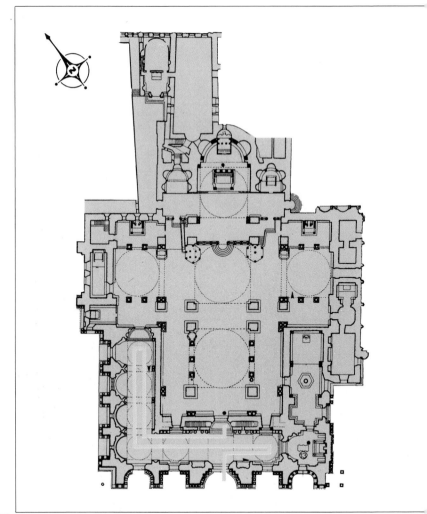

of Genesis and Exodus and largely based on the miniatures in an early Christian Alexandrian bible (the Cotton Bible), begins in the south-western corner on the right and continues along the west and north sides.

The first is the cupola of the *Creation*, geometrically divided into three concentric circular bands around a gilded scale decoration in the centre.

The story is divided into 26 scenes, above which runs a biblical text in Latin starting with the words "In the beginning God created the heaven and the earth. And the Spirit of God moved upon the face of the waters."

Next follow the days of the creation. Each shows the

9) Atrium, west side. The upper part of the walls is covered with mosaics; the lower part with precious marble, columns and capitals from Constantinople.

9

On page 32

10) West atrium, Creation Cupola. The creation of the world is narrated in 26 scenes enclosed in 3 concentric bands. (13th century).

figure of God the Creator, identified in accordance with Oriental iconography in the young Christ with a crossed halo and a processional cross, living Word of the Father and with Him, from the beginning, Creator of the universe, as recounted at the start of St. John's Gospel.

The six days of the Creation are recounted in the scenes portrayed in the two innermost bands. In the first, God divides the light from the darkness, in the second He divides the waters which were under the firmament from the waters which were above the firmament, in the third He makes the earth bring forth every species of plant, in the fourth He sets the sun and moon in the firmament of heaven to rule the day and the night, in the fifth He populates the waters with fish and the sky with winged fowl and creates the animals of the earth, here shown in pairs — first the lions, then the tigers, leopards, elephants, asses and all the others — and in the sixth God says "Let us make man in our image, after our likeness".

In each scene, the figure of an angel is shown alongside the work of the Creator.

The scene of the *Blessing of the Seventh day* is of great interest because it is uncommon in portrayals of the Creation. Here God, seated on a throne surrounded by the six angels of the first six days as if in a royal

Abraham gathers the three Angels together.

Stories of Abraham.

Stories of Noah - Building of the Ark and the Universal Diluvium.

The Dome of the Creation.

Left Arm of the Atrium.

Stories of Noah: The condemnation of Cam, The Tower of Babel.

11/12) West atrium, Creation Cupola.

Top
Detail of 1st day: *God separates light from darkness* (13th century).

Bottom
Detail of 5th day: *God creates the animals of the earth* (13th century).

▶

13) West atrium, Creation cupola. Detail of 6th day: *God makes Adam* (13th century).

court, lays His hand in blessing on the seventh ange representing the Sabbath, which God reserved f Himself. Above are the biblical words "*And Go blessed the seventh day*".

Below, *the creation of Eve from Adam's rib, th temptation by the serpent, Adam and Eve disobedience to God's commands* and *the banishme from the garden of Eden* conclude the lower band the cupola.

The cherubim set by God to guard the garden Eden are portrayed in the pendentives below.

On the surrounding arches and lunettes, near Clement's door, the bible story continues with *t birth of Cain and Abel* and *Cain's crime*, th beginning of an evil which was to be rampant amor

11

12

34

14/15) West atrium, Creation Cupola.
Top. Detail of 7th day: *The blessing of the 7th day, which God reserved for Himself* (13th century).
Bottom. Detail of the *creation of Eve* (13th century).

16/17) West atrium. Soffit with *stories of Noah and the Flood.* (13th century).
Top. *Noah makes the ark to shelter the animals and his family.* (13h century)
Bottom. Detail of the *Flood* (13th century).

men until their total destruction in the flood. Only Noah, the just man, his family and the animals he chose were to be saved (soffit towards central portal). *The stories of Noah* continue in the next soffit beyond the portal, which also depicts *the building of the Tower of Babel* and *the condemnation of human pride.*

In the other cupolas of the atrium the scenes develop in a single uninterrupted strip at the base.

The second cupola and the lunette near St. Peter's door tell the *story of Abraham*, ancestor of a race chosen by God for salvation. God talking to Abraham is portrayed by a hand issuing forth from a segment of sky. The scene is repeated four times, and divides the sequence of the story into four parts.

14

15

16

17

18) West atrium. Soffit with *stories of Noah and the Flood.* Detail (13th century).

19) West atrium. Soffit to the left of the main portal. *The building of the Tower of Babel.* Detail (13th century).

The next three cupolas depict *the stories of Joseph the Jew*, the interpreter of dreams. After being unjustly condemned he found favour with the Pharaoh and became the saviour of the people of Egypt, and of the brothers who had betrayed him.

The decoration of the atrium concludes with a flourish in the Moses cupola, the masterpiece of the last generation of 13th-century Venetian mosaicists. The scenes follow without interruption, rich in figures which are no longer individually silhouetted in gold but inserted in various natural spaces and magnificent architecture. They portray *the story of Moses* who was saved from the waters of the Nile to become the saviour and guide of his people through the desert and across the Red Sea to the Promised Land. Moses

18

the figure of Jesus, the Saviour of all mankind, shown in the arms of the Virgin Mary between the Evangelists Mark and John in the mosaic of the semi-dome above the nearby door.

Returning to the main door, the Gothic tomb of Bartolomeo Recovrati (d. 1420), the tomb of Doge Marino Morosini (d. 1253) which re-used an early Christian relief panel, and the Gothic tomb of Doge Bartolomeo Gradenigo (d. 1342) can be seen on the right between the arches.

On the right of the main portal is the entrance to "**St. Mark's Museum**", founded at the end of the 19th century and currently housed in the areas above the north-west atrium. It contains objects of various kinds belonging to the Basilica. *The Horses of St. Mark,*

20) North atrium. 2nd cupola with *stories of Joseph* (13th century).

21) North atrium. 3rd cupola with *stories of Joseph* (13th century).

22/23) St. Mark's Museum. "Pala feriale" by Paolo Veneziano (14th century).

Bottom

Detail of upper register: *St. Peter*

Side

Detail of lower register: *St. Mark saves the sailors from shipwreck* (14th century).

moved from their traditional position at the centre of the main façade after the last restoration, which revealed their splendid original gilding, were recently housed here. They are the only example in the world of multiple equestrian sculpture of the Classical period (it is not known whether they are of Greek or Roman manufacture). The Horse Room also contains the "pala feriale" by Paolo Veneziano, a wooden panel dating from the mid-14th century painted with stories of St. Mark, once used to cover the *Pala d'oro*. The Museum contains Persian carpets dating from the early 17th century, precious liturgical vestments, illuminated manuscripts from the 15th and 16th centuries with the text of Mark's liturgy, and fragments of ancient mosaics which became

22

24) St. Mark's Museum: *the Horses of St. Mark*. The gilded bronze quadriga was brought to Venice from Constantinople after 1204. The sculptor is unknown; some experts believe it to be a Hellenistic and others a Roman work.

detached during the 19th century restoration. The Museum also houses 15th century wool tapestries portraying *stories of the Passion of Jesus* and others dating from the 16th century, including silk and silver tapestries depicting stories from the life of St. Mark.

25) St. Mark's Museum. Fragment of mosaic belonging to *The Massacre of the Innocents* in the antebaptistry (14th century).

26) St. Mark's Museum. Fragment of mosaic detached from the right-hand tribune in the presbytery. *The pious women* (11th century).

26

Understanding the mosaics

The mosaic decoration which covers the entire upper part of the architecture of St. Mark's over an area of some 8000 square metres, apparently fragmented between numerous scenes and individual figures, is actually based on a unified concept which ancient tradition attributes to Gioachino da Fiore, a Calabrian monk with a prophetic spirit who lived in Venice in the late 12th century.

Experts now agree that the great iconographic plan of the interior, already designed in the 12th century, was devised by an unknown Venetian theologian, freely inspired by Byzantine models.

The orientation of the Basilica, with the presbytery facing east and the main door west in accordance with traditional canons, indicates the axis or route of the sun along which the main nucleus of the ancient mosaics should be followed. This route recounts the story of the salvation brought to men by Jesus, Sun of the world which never sets.

It begins with the presbytery cupola, also called the cupola of the prophets, each of whom is portrayed alongside his prophecy relating to the Messiah, the Christ Emmanuel of the central circle.

The Virgin Mary is among them with her hands outstretched to welcome the annunciated Son, representing the link between the Old and New Covenants.

The five scenes in the next vault - the Annunciation, the Adoration of the Magi, the Presentation in the Temple, the Baptism, and the Transfiguration in the centre - recount the fulfilment of the prophecies, and the beginning of Jesus of Nazareth's historical presence among men.

The deeds performed by Jesus to comfort the suffering, the sick and sinners are portrayed on the walls and the vaults of the two transepts, starting with the miracle of the wedding of Cana (north vault of central cupola).

The scenes relating to the last moments of Jesus' life bring us back to the central cupola, which celebrates the glory of His ascension to Heaven.

The third cupola to the west celebrates Pentecost, when the Holy Ghost descended on the apostles, moving them to carry the Gospel to all the people and to found the Church among men. The Last Coming, when Christ returns as Judge, is portrayed in the two western vaults of the Apocalypse and Heaven.

The mosaics in the atrium, added later in the 13th century, with their meditation on the Old Testament in general and the books of Genesis and Exodus in particular, are well placed as a foretaste of the interior.

Interwoven with this main plan are many others, including stories of the Virgin Mary (in the two transepts), the martyrdom of St. Peter and St. Clement (in the Chapels dedicated to them), the lives of St. John the evangelist (in the north transept), John the Baptist (in the Baptistry) and St. Isidore (in the Chapel named after him), the great pantheon of saints venerated by the Venetians (in the soffits of the entire basilica), and most important of all, the cycles portraying the legend of St. Mark. Finally, the gold in which the visitor feels enwrapped when gazing up at the mosaics, not only represents a lustrous background which unifies all the mosaic work but also, in accordance with the Byzantine concept, has a specific symbolic value in St. Mark, as the colour of the Divine and the image of the Light which, to Mediaeval theologians and fathers of the Church, was God Himself.

28) West atrium. St. Clement's door made of damascened pinchbeck with figures of saints and prophets. Byzantine manufacture (12th century).

The Interior

The interior is reached through the **main door**, made of an ancient alloy similar to brass known as orichalc damaskeened with figures of saints and prophets as mediators. The door, made in the 12th century in Byzantium, has inscribed upon it the name of the Venetian Leo da Molin, procurator of San Marco between 1110 and 1120, for whom it was made and who is shown genuflecting before St. Mark. This valuable door was modelled on the older Byzantine door of St. Clement on the right.

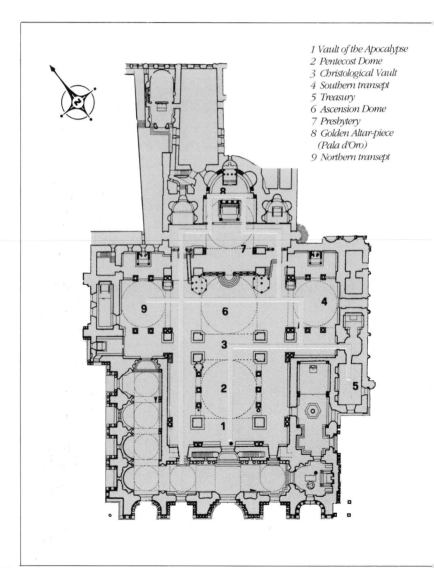

1 Vault of the Apocalypse
2 Pentecost Dome
3 Christological Vault
4 Southern transept
5 Treasury
6 Ascension Dome
7 Presbytery
8 Golden Altar-piece
  (Pala d'Oro)
9 Northern transept

29) West atrium. In the centre of the main portal is the great damascened pinchbeck door with the figures of Christ, the Virgin Mary, saints and prophets with the function of intercessors (12th century); around it are niches with the Virgin Mary among the apostles and evangelists (among the oldest mosaics, dating from the 11th and 12th centuries), and above it, an imposing St. Mark in liturgical vestments (16th century).

Around the door in niches of various sizes are mosaic figures of the Virgin Mary and Child amongst eight apostles (upper register) and the four evangelists (lower register). These are perhaps the oldest mosaics in the basilica, made at the end of the 11th century by Byzantine masters who brought the art of mosaic to Venice.

The inscriptions around the niches of the evangelists are interesting. They are two leonine verses in mediaeval Latin, divided into four hemistichs, which translate into English as follows: "These four hemistichs are "sentinels" of the Church of Christ/ their sweet canto resounds and moves through every part of heaven". Reading the inscriptions accompanying the mosaics strengthens their

29

significance as a holy text open to believers. All the scenes are accompanied by a Latin text taken mainly from the books of the Old and New Testaments, but sometimes they are mediaeval prayers and invocations. The individual figures of the saints also have their names beside them and the numerous images of Jesus and the Virgin Mary have their Greek monograms.

Beyond the door and entering the sacred area of the basilica, the gilded mosaics which surround the upper architecture are certainly the most interesting aspect for the sense of unity they give to the interior and their Byzantine references, such as the symbolic meaning of the gold which is the colour of heaven.

Before setting off on the route which will take us to

30) Interior of the Basilica. View of the main nave towards the presbytery.

30

some of the most important elements of the mosaic and sculptural decoration, it is interesting to look at the architectural structure. As has already been mentioned, St. Mark's Basilica is in the shape of a Greek cross, with the longitudinal nave slightly longer than the transepts. The five large domes of the structure repeat the unique design seen in the central dome, with its pendentives and large vaults resting on four pillars. These pillars are divided into four "feet" which support the interior, with a second level of small domed vaults forming a cupolino.

The symbolic importance attributed to the spaces is also of Byzantine origin. Under the semicircular domes, representing heaven and separated by the light that enters at the bottom through the windows,

31) Lunette above the main door. *Deesis* (prayer of intercession): Christ enthroned between the Virgin Mary and St. Mark (13th century).

32) General view towards the south transept.

33) General view: vaults under the central Ascension Cupola (12th century mosaics).

33

34) Pentecost Cupola: the Holy Ghost, portrayed in the centre in the form of a dove, descends like fire on the apostles. The peoples who listened to the apostles' preaching, each in their own language, are portrayed between the windows (12th century).

34

35) South wall of the central nave. **The Prayer at the Mount of Olives.** In three successive scenes, masterpieces by three different masters portray the sorrowful, lonely prayer of Jesus (13th century).

there is a symbolic quadrangular space symbolising terrestrial reality. The walls of this lower part of the building are decorated with oriental marble, the longitudinal cut of which highlights the repetitive design of the grain, creating the effect of a valuable damask.

The columns, topped by sculpted and gilded capitals, are extremely beautiful; their dates and places of origin vary.

The route the visitor may follow, though limited, allows one an excellent opportunity to investigate the most important mosaic and sculptural elements of the church.

Above the entrance, the **Apocalypse and the Paradise vaults** - the latter also visible from the atrium through the "well" opening - are decorated

35

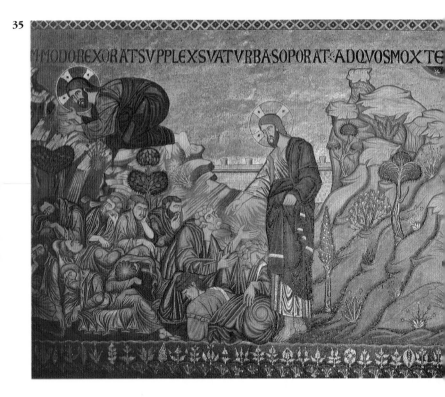

with Renaissance mosaics which were largely restored in the 19th century. Depicting the apocalyptic visions of John and the Final Judgement these scenes represent the spiritual message contained in the mosaics (see the insert on page 48). In the following **dome**, known as the **Pentecost,** the Holy Spirit, in the form of a dove in the centre descends upon the apostles as tongues of fire. Below

between the windows, are the people who,
according to the New Testament, listened to the
sermon of the apostles, each in their own language
(Acts 2, 7-11). In the **pendentives**, four great angels
sing the hymn of glory: "Holy, holy, holy is the Lord"
(mosaics from the mid-12th century).

On the two vaults at the sides of the dome are *the
apostle martyrs*. The one on the right is still in its
original mediaeval form, whilst the one on the left
was restored in the 17th century.

These and other replacements were necessary
because of damage to the mosaics due to dampness,
fires and earthquakes, documented in ancient
chronicles.

On the walls of the right aisle *the Sermon on the
Mount of Olives* (1215-1220) is a masterpiece in which

the hand of three masters can be identified. To each is
attributed one of the three scenes telling of the painful and
solitary prayer of Christ, the indifference of his friends is
expressed in the group of sleepers on the left.

Further below the "pinakes", elegant mosaic pictures by the
same artists, depict the *Virgin Mary* and four *prophets*, with
Christ Emanuel and another four *Prophets* on the opposite
wall.

In the wall is the entrance to the **baptistry** (see page 88).

Following the proposed route, one passes beneath the **Christological vault** between the Pentecost and Ascension domes. In subsequent domes on the right and left the final moments of the life of Jesus are depicted: *The Kiss of Judas, The Sentence of Pontius Pilate, The Crucifixion, Women at the Sepulcre, Descent into Limbo* and *Meeting with Thomas*. The whole of the vault (except for the central picture, which is a 15th century restoration) was painted in the second half of the 12th century and despite numerous restorations, still appears as an integral piece.

The south transept is the area closest to the Doge's

36) Christological Vault. *Pilate condemns Jesus to death* (12th century).

37/38) South and north walls of the central nave: the "Pinakes". The Virgin Mary and Christ Emmanuel are portrayed at the centre among eight prophets (13th century).

37 **38**

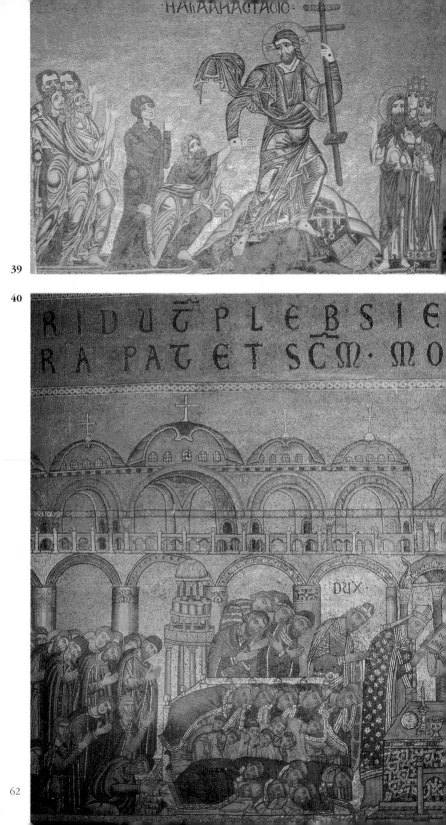

39

40

Palace, to which it is connected by a door giving the Doge direct access to the basilica.

The dome is all gold and depicts four saints (*Leonardo, Nicola, Clemente, Biagio*) who are considered special protectors of the state, together with the saints from the tradition of Grado depicted in the pendentives (*Dorotea, Eufemia, Erasma, Tecla*).

On the west wall is a mosaic from about 1220 depicting two scenes of *The Miracle of the Discovery of the Body of St. Mark*, which was lost during the construction of the third basilica in 1094.

Through a door with a marvellous Moorish-style arch above it one reaches the **Treasury**, which is divided into three sections: the entrance, the sanctuary and

39) Christological Vault.
The *Anastasis* or *Descent to Limbo* portrays Jesus victorious over death and the devil (12th century).

40) South transept, wall facing the altar. *The miracle of the rediscovery of St. Mark's body* (13th century).

41) Chalice of the emperor Romanos, Byzantine setting with cloisonné enamel (10th century).

42) Reliquary of St. George's arm made of gilded silver and enamel (13th-15th century, Venetian art).

the treasury. In the sanctuary there are eight niche with numerous valuable reliquaries containin famous relics of saints collected, as was the habit mediaeval times, from Constantinople, the Holy Lar and different places from the eastern Mediterranean. The Treasury brings together 283 pieces in gol silver and glass and other valuable materials fron various sources. This is what remains of the Treasur of the Republic plundered after its fall in 1797 an impoverished by the sale of precious gems and pear between 1815 and 1819 in order to restore th basilica. The most interesting part of the collection a objects brought to Venice from Constantinople afte 1204. These were mainly liturgical chalices, goble and patens in semiprecious stone mounted o

41

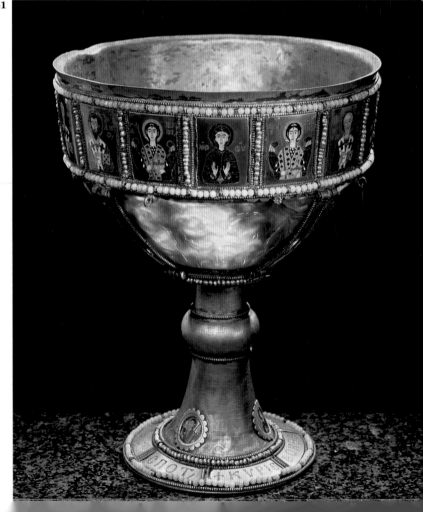

43) Gilded silver perfume burner or processional lamp in the shape of a building surmounted by cupolas (12th century, made in southern Italy or perhaps in Venice).

44) Icon of the archangel Michael made of gilded enamel and silver (11th century, Byzantine art).

enamelled Byzantine goldwork. Two icons of the archangel Michael with enamelled frames are also part of the collection. In addition, there are vases in glass and semiprecious stone from late antiquity and goblets with an Islamic provenance, all of which are of great interest. Finally, there is a collection of western objects, including filigree works from Venice. Returning to the church, on the vault between the dome of the south transept and the one of Ascension are the four episodes from the life of Christ: *The Temptation, Entry into Jerusalem, The Last Supper* and *Washing the Disciples' Feet* (some of the best conserved mosaics from the first half of the 12th century).

43

45/46) South vault of the Ascension Cupola: *The Last Supper* and *The Washing of the Feet* (12th century).

47) South vault of Ascension Cupola. Detail.

From the centre of the basilica, beneath the **dome of the Ascension**, some of the architectural modifications can be clearly seen, such as the two large Gothic **windows** to the south towards the Doge's Palace and to the west towards the square, and some additional sculptures, such as the Gothic **iconostasis** with 14 beautiful statues (*12 apostles* with the *Virgin Mary* and *St.Mark*) on either side of the Crucifix, the work of the Venetian brothers Pierpaolo and Jacobello Masagne (1394), and the small Renaissance **altars** of *St. Paul* and *St. James* against the pillars.

To the sides of the iconostasis are, to the left, the **double pulpit** for liturgical readings, with clearly Byzantine influences, and to the right, an octagonal

45

46

preceding page
48) Central Ascension Cupola: the glorification of Jesus Christ as told in the Acts of the apostles (12th century).
The "Festa della Sensa", the most famous political and religious feast of the Venetian state, was celebrated on Ascension Day.

pulpit in porphyry, held up by nine columns an- formerly reserved for the Doge in certain officia ceremonies.

The mosaic decoration of the dome, from the secon- half of the 12th century, is a masterpiece of the S Mark's mosaics and the heart of the spiritual messag- of the basilica. In the centre, Christ sitting on rainbow is held up by four flying angels. Beneath this, in a large concentric circle, the Virgin Mar- between two angels and the twelve apostles all loo- upwards, alternating between majolica jars of varyin- shapes and sizes suggesting the Mount of Olive- where Luke places the Ascension (Acts 1,12). Lowe- down, between the windows at the bottom of th- dome, 16 female figures depict *The Virtues and th-*

49

Beatitudes. On the pendentives, *the four evangelists* are writing the start of the Gospel and the four biblical rivers - **Gion, Fison, the Tigris and the Euphrates** - pour their waters onto the faithful, clearly symbolising the baptism.

The **Presbytery** is the area beyond the iconostasis which by ancient tradition is reserved for the clergy during liturgical celebrations. It was here that the seat of the Doge was situated. Access is from the right, through the Chapel of St.Clement.

In the centre, above **the tomb of St. Mark**, the baldachin in old green marble, supported by four columns in alabaster decorated with historical scenes from the Gospel (13th century), covers **the main altar** in the form taken on in the last century, when

49) Gothic iconostasis by Pierpaolo and Jacobello dalle Masegne. Around the Crucifix are the 12 apostles with the Virgin Mary and St. Mark (14th century).

50) Presbytery. The high altar contains the urn with the relics of St. Mark's body. It is covered by a precious verd antique marble ciborium supported by four sculpted alabaster columns (13th century).

51) Presbytery. Ciborium column. Detail.

the **tomb** was moved here from its old site in the crypt.

In the presbytery are bronze sculptures by Jacopo Sansovino, who was responsible for the conservation of the basilica (see photo) between 1529 and 1570 including the **pulpits** near the iconostasis with the miracles of St. Mark, **the statues of the four evangelists** on the two balustrades, **the tabernacle** of the small altar behind the gold altar-piece and **the door to the sacristy** (a Renaissance room from the end of the 15th century with a mosaic vault and wooden decorations on the walls, partly inlaid).

From the centre of the presbytery **the vaults of the two chancels** can be clearly seen, decorated with mosaics from the 12th century and greatly restored in

50

52) Presbytery. Right-hand chancel. *The abduction of St. Mark's body from Alexandria* (12th century).

53) Presbytery. The prophets' Cupola: around the figure of the Virgin Mary 13 prophets announce the coming of the Messiah, portrayed in the centre (12th century).

54) Presbytery. Semi-dome of apse: Christ, Lord of the universe (restored in 1506).

the 19th century. These recount episodes of *the Life of St. Mark* (left), the *Abduction of the body of the saint from Alexandria in Egypt* and its *arrival in Venice* (right).

In the middle is **the dome of the prophets** (12th century with restorations). Around the Virgin Mary thirteen prophets display the scrolls of their Messianic prophecies.

On the **vault of the apse** is a large *Christ the Almighty*, Lord of the universe. This is a restoration of 1506 by a master Renaissance mosaic artist of the original Byzantine-style image. Below, four persons particularly revered by the Venetians (*Nicola, Pietro, Marco, Ermagora*) are depicted. These are very old mosaics (from the end of the 11th century or the start

52

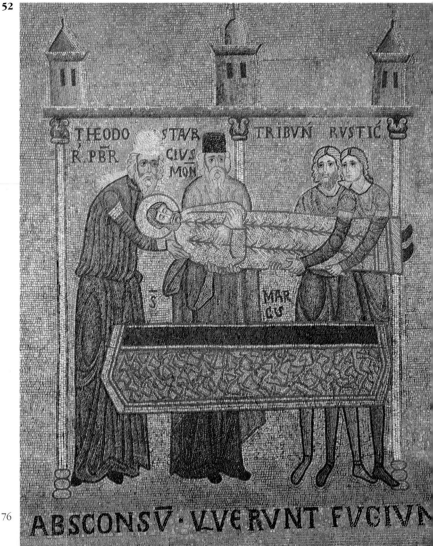

53

54

55) The Pala d'oro. Cloisonné enamels on gold leaf (10th-12th century Byzantine manufacture) in a gilded silver frame with pearls and precious stones (14th century Venetian Gothic work).

of the 12th century), though they have undergone a number of modern restorations.

Behind the main altar, the **gold altar-piece** has remained in its original position. It is an altar-piece with about 250 *cloisonnés* enamel paintings on gold foil of varying sizes and from varying periods (10th-12th centuries), made in Byzantium for Venetian clients. In the lower picture, around the Almighty, at the centre are the evangelists, prophets, apostles and angels. The small surrounding panels show episodes from the life of Christ and St. Mark. The Gothic frame in gilded silver was made in Venice in the mid-14th century (during the dogeship of Andrea Dandolo). Numerous pearls and precious stones are set in the enamel. The gold altar-piece is the only example in

55

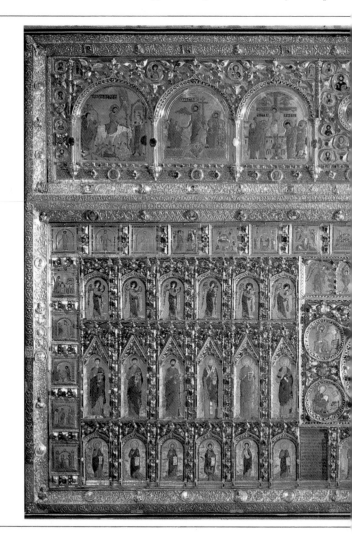

the world of Gothic gold-work of any size that has remained in one piece.

Crossing **the Chapel of St. Peter** one descends to **the north transept**, dedicated to *St. John the evangelist* (the mosaics of the 12th century dome show apocryphal episodes from the life of the saint), and the *Madonna* (the 12th century mosaics on the vault and the west wall with the stories of Mary and the childhood of Christ are inspired by apocryphal stories). On the north wall is the large genealogical tree of the Virgin Mary, with the Infant Jesus at the top, and a 16th century insertion.

Since 1617, when the existing altar was built, the *Madonna Nicopeia* has been on display, a Byzantine icon that has always been greatly revered by

following page
56) Presbytery. The Pala d'oro. Detail of the upper part: the archangel Michael.

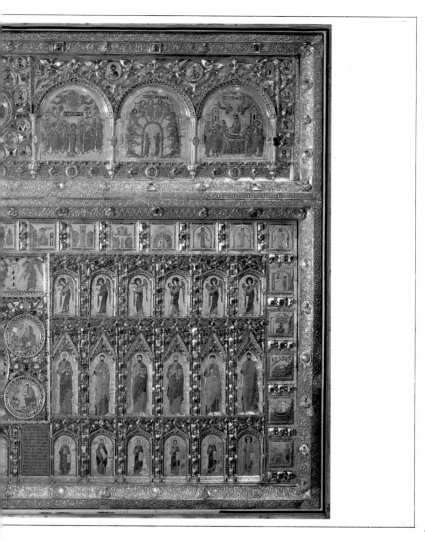

57

59

Venetians.

From the north transept one gains access to **the Chapel of St. Isidore** and to the **Mascoli Chapel** (see pp. 99 and 104).

Along the aisle towards the exit (**St. Peter's door**) one can see part of the ancient marble **floor**, a beautiful example of different techniques, mainly "opus sectile" (geometric shapes).

Animals are also depicted (peacocks, eagles, doves, chickens, foxes), a reference to ancient mediaeval symbolism.

The floor, which originally covered the whole of the

57) North transept. The Madonna Nicopeia altar (17th century).

58) North transept. The Madonna Nicopeia, a Byzantine icon greatly venerated by the Venetians.

59) North transept. The family tree of the Virgin Mary or tree of Jesse, her ancestor. The Madonna and Child are portrayed at the top (16th century).

60) Floor plan, designed for the first time by Antonio Visentini (18th century).

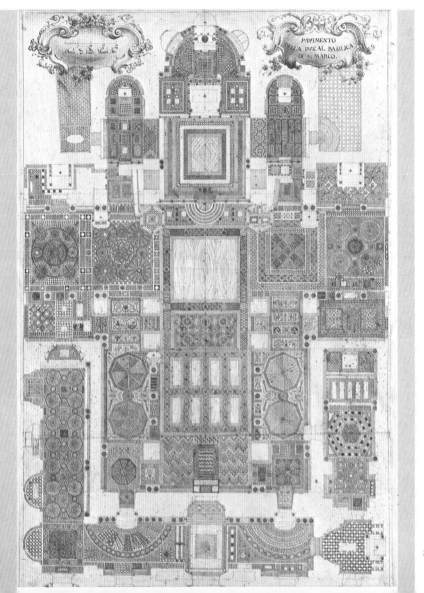

preceding page
61) Floor. Detail of the north transept.

62) Floor. Detail of tridimensional decoration in front of St. Peter's door, after a design by Paolo Uccello (15th century).

63) Floor. Detail of the central nave with large "proconnesio" marble slabs.

basilica like a great oriental carpet, highlights, both in the atrium and the interior, the focal points of the architectural structure. Down the centuries it has been restored many times and many pieces have been replaced due to the fragile nature of the material and the wear and tear that it has always been subject to.

62

The Chapels

The Baptistry

The nave leads to the **baptistry** on the southern side of the basilica.

This Chapel was built in the first half of the 14th century and occupies an area considered to have been an old open archway between the Doge's Palace and the church.

The mosaic decoration was created on two levels, one in relation to the figure of John the Baptist and the other centred on the baptism, the means of

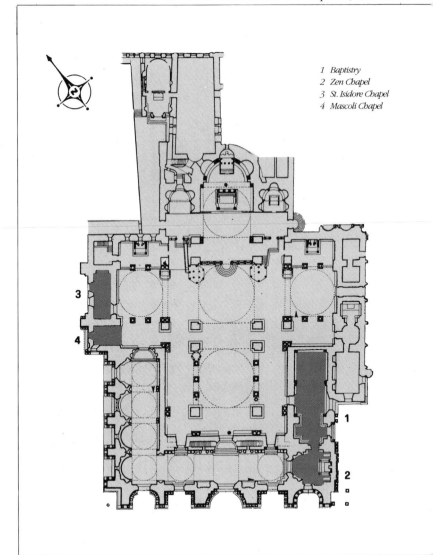

1 Baptistry
2 Zen Chapel
3 St. Isidore Chapel
4 Mascoli Chapel

salvation that Christ brought to humanity. This was the wish of the Doge, Andrea Dandolo (1343-1354), one of the most illustrious Doges of the Republic, a historian and friend of Petrarch, depicted genuflecting at the foot of the cross in the great scene of the Crucifixion behind the altar.

The tomb of Dandolo, the last Doge buried in the basilica, is to be found along the external wall and is a Gothic monument of very fine execution.

The baptistry is subdivided into three areas, the logical progression of which is best appreciated by entering the antebaptistry through the small square towards the wharf. This passage is rectangular and

64) Baptistry. General view. On the right is the Gothic tomb of Doge Andrea Dandolo (d. 1354). Centre: the baptismal font surmounted by the statue of John the Baptist (16th century).

following page
65) Baptistry. Cupola above the font: *Jesus sends the apostles world-wide to baptise* (14th century).

64

66) Antebaptistry. *The baptism of Jesus* (14th century).

67) Baptistry. Lunette above the altar: *Christ crucified between the Virgin Mary and St. Mark* on the one side and *St. John the evangelist and St. John the Baptist* on the other. Kneeling at His feet is Doge A. Dandolo (14th century).

68) Baptistry. Lunette above the door towards the church: *the dance of Salomé*. Detail (14th century).

covered by a barrel vault depicting prophets from the Old Testament. On the walls below, episodes from the childhood of Jesus intertwine with those of the life of John the Baptist and in the picture in front of the door the *Baptism of Jesus in the Jordan* is modelled on Byzantine iconographic canons. These mosaics have a clear didactic intention for those waiting to be baptised.

In the antebaptistry, there is another much simpler Gothic tomb, where the Doge Giovanni Soranzo (1312-1328) is buried.

The following two square rooms are the baptistry proper and the presbytery. In the middle of the former is a beautiful christening font with a bronze bas-relief cover by Jacopo Sansovino, who is buried

66

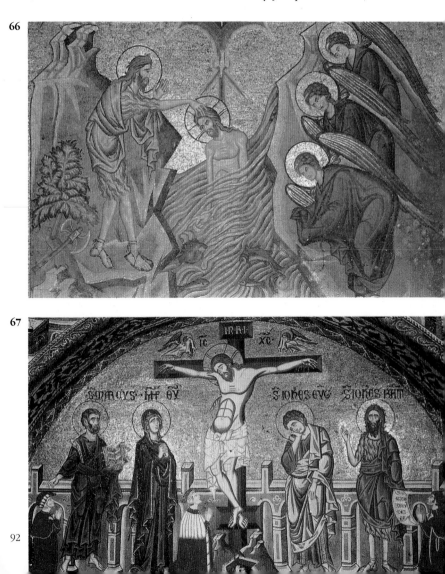

67

69) Baptistry. Lunette on the left of the altar: *the beheading and deposition of John the Baptist* (14th century).

in the Chapel, and his pupils. Above is a bronze statue of John the Baptist.

In the dome above, Jesus sends the apostles worldwide to preach and baptise. The places in which they preached are recorded in the inscriptions.

In the dome of the small presbytery, Christ in his glory amongst the nine angelic hierarchies is depicted in an iconography that is still very close to Byzantine influences.

From the lunette on the right the stories of John the Baptist begin with the *Announcement to Zachariah* and the *Meeting between Zachariah and Elisabeth* and continue along the walls ending on the left above the door towards the church and in the next

lunette with the *dance of Salome and the Martyrdom
of the saint*, two works of extraordinary beauty by the
last mediaeval Venetian mosaic artists.

70) Zen Chapel. Renaissance sculptural complex of the altar: *Madonna and Child between St. Peter and St. John the Baptist* (16th century).

71) Dome mosaics (13th century). *St. Mark's dream.*

72) Dome mosaics (13th century). *St. Mark taken prisoner.*

73) Dome mosaics (13th century). *The martyrdom of St. Mark.*

The Zen Chapel

The **Zen Chapel** is entered either through the baptistry or the atrium through a beautiful old bronze door with small arches (5th-6th centuries), taken to Venice from Constantinople.

In ancient times this south-western corner was the vestibule of the "sea door". The 13th-century mosaic on the vault and the older ones above the portal document its original function as an important entrance. On the vault there are twelve scenes o stories of St. Mark in two registers. On the semi-dome above the portal, the Virgin and Child is between two worshipping angels and further up there are eight prophets (four are beautiful Romanesque sculpture

70

71

72

73

74) Zen Chapel. Mosaics on the vault with stories of St. Mark. Detail of martyrdom (13th century)

in marble and the other four are mosaics).

Only at the start of the 16th century was the large arch towards the outside closed to build the funeral Chapel for Cardinal Giovanni Battista Zen a recompense for a considerable bequest from him to the state.

The Renaissance sculptures are also from this period their design and partial realisation by Antonio Lombardo. The bronze combination of the altar is made up of a rich baldachin with a statue of the Virgin Mary beneath it - her golden shoe relating to the legend of the miraculous transformation of a shoe offered by a poor Christian - between St. Peter and John the Baptist.

At the centre, on the bronze monumental

74

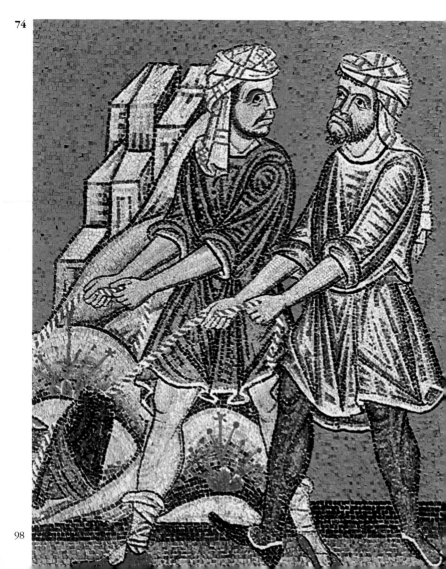

sarcophagus is a representation of Giovanni Battista Zen in the gowns of Cardinal. At the side are six richly decorated feminine figures of virtue.

The Chapel of St. Isidore

The **Chapel of St. Isidore**, situated at the side of the north transept has the simple shape of a rectangle covered by a barrel vault entirely covered in mosaics. Built as the baptistry for the Doge Andrea Dandolo, it was completed on 10th July 1355, as the inscription on the lunette above the altar states.
The Chapel can only be visited at certain limited times.

75) St. Isidore's Chapel

following page
76) St. Isidore's Chapel. Lunette above the altar: *Christ enthroned between St. Mark and St. Isidore*. Below, a long inscription contains the names of the Doges and procurators of St. Mark who presided over the building of the Chapel (14th century).

75

IC

S MAR
CV.

+ CORꝑBTLꝰ SIDORI PꝶTIARHA QLAꝩ
QLITꝰ VENEĊ DVĊEI ꝺꝺ CⱵ XXꝩ Qꝶꝺ C
NEM EDIFICAĊIOIS Hꝩꝺ APELE Sꝩꝺ
Lꝺꝺ ꝺ QLITꝺ VENEĊ DꝩĊE 7 TPR NO
ꝶꝑꝺꝺꝩ Rꝩ Qꝺ Ŝ MRĊꝺ 7 ꝐꝩEĊTA Oꝩ
NOBꝺꝺ ꝩ VꝺROꝪ DNOꝪ MꝶĊꝺ LAꝩ REDꝺ̇ꝺꝺ

XC

:SYSI
DOR

ECCDEYÆTA·OHO·P·DNX·DNAÜ·MICHAELI·IN
AIECC·S·MARCI·PMASIT·VSOZ·AD·ICEPCIO
DHIFICAT·I·CEPT·DVCATE·DNO·AITREGA·DADY
OX·DNORZ·MARCILAYRADMO·7·IOHX·DELPHI
TO·IOHÆ·GDOICHO·ICLIMT·VENGDVCE·7·TPR
IA·IO·7·IOHX·DELPHI·IN·PQVSZ·ECOAS·HABOIIM

77) St. Isidore's Chapel
Lunette on the back wall.
Madonna and Child between
St. John the Baptist and St.
Nicholas, detail (14th century).

The wall that the altar backs on to is decorated with
valuable marble from Greece. At the sides, above two
small shelves, two elegant figures represent the
Annunciation. Above the marble tomb the figure of
St. Isidore is sculpted, watched over by an incense
bearing angel. The front of the sarcophagus, at one
time gilded, has a bas-relief of the martyrdom of the
saint between the figures of Christ, St. Mark and St.
Isidore. The mosaics of the vault tell the story in two
rows of episodes from the life of St. Isidore on the

77

island of Chios and the transportation of the body of the saint to Venice in 1125 by the Doge Domenico Michiel. On the lunette above the altar are: *Christ between St. Mark and St. Isidore*; on the opposite wall: *The Virgin Mary between John the Baptist and St. Nicholas*.

The mosaics of the two lunettes are linked to the Byzantine iconographic tradition, whereas the realistic narration in the stories of St. Isidore is more open to western influence.

78) St. Isidore's Chapel. Mosaics on the vault with stories of St. Isidore. *The saint baptising at Chios* (14th century).

78

79) The Mascoli Chapel.

80) Mascoli Chapel. Detail of the *Annunciation* scene (15th century)

The Mascoli Chapel

The construction of the Nove or Madonna Chapel was begun in 1430, during the dogeship of Francesco Foscari, as can be read in the inscriptions above the altar. This was probably a reconstruction of a space that served as a vestibule for the Chapel of St. Isidore, where a bricked-up communication door is still visible. The name of the **Mascoli Chapel**, as it is commonly known, arose in 1618 when its use was connected to the Mascoli confraternity.

On the end wall is a marble altar formed of three narrow shell-shaped niches separated by spiral columns holding the Virgin and Child between St. Mark and St. John. The Gothic elegance of these statues recalls other sculptures inside the basilica.

The mosaic decoration of the vault and the end wall

79

preceding page
81) Mascoli Chapel. Back wall: *the Annunciation* (15th century).

82) Mascoli Chapel. *The Death of the Virgin* concludes the storie of the Virgin Mary on the vaults.

83) General view of crypt after restoration, 1987-1993. The crypt, a huge 9th-century room below the presbytery, is the heart of the Basilica because it contains the votive chapel in which the body of St. Mark lay until the early 19th century. Since 1835, St. Mark's body has rested under the mensa of the high haltar.

is a result of the original dedication of the Chapel to the Virgin Mary. These show the canonical episodes of her life starting from the left: *The Birth, The Presentation in the Temple, The Annunciation, The Visitation, The Death.*

The two semibarrel vaults display an interesting difference in the architecture of the scene. The Venetian Gothic style of the buildings on the left contrasts with the Tuscan Renaissance setting in which the two episodes depicted on the right are found. Around the middle of the 15th century, a Venetian artist (Michele Giambono), who was responsible for the models of the two first scenes, was replaced - it is not known why - by a Tuscan painter (perhaps Andrea del Castagno) present in Venice.

82

INDEX